LEADING
WOMEN

Benazir Bhutto

CORINNE J. NADEN

mc Marshall Benchmark
New York

Other Marshall Cavendish Offices:
Marshall Cavendish International (Asia) Private Limited, 1 New Industrial Road, Singapore 536196 • Marshall
Cavendish International (Thailand) Co Ltd. 253 Asoke, 12th Flr, Sukhumvit 21 Road, Klongtoey Nua, Wattana,
Bangkok 10110, Thailand • Marshall Cavendish (Malaysia) Sdn Bhd, Times Subang, Lot 46, Subang Hi-Tech Industrial
Park, Batu Tiga, 40000 Shah Alam, Selangor Darul Ehsan, Malaysia
Marshall Cavendish is a trademark of Times Publishing Limited

All websites were available and accurate when this book was sent to press.

Library of Congress Cataloging-in-Publication Data
Naden, Corinne J.
Benazir Bhutto / by Corinne J. Naden.
p. cm. — (Leading women)
Includes bibliographical references and index.
Summary: "Presents the biography of Benazir Bhutto against the backdrop of
her political, historical, and cultural environment"—Provided by publisher.
ISBN 978-0-7614-4952-2
1. Bhutto, Benazir—Juvenile literature. 2. Women prime
ministers—Pakistan—Biography—Juvenile literature.
3. Primeministers—Pakistan—Biography—Juvenile literature. 4. Pakistan—Politics
and government—1988—Juvenile literature. I. Title.
DS389.22.B48N34 2010
954.9105'2092—dc22 [B]
2009029654

Editor: Deborah Grahame   Art Director: Anahid Hamparian
Publisher: Michelle Bisson   Series Designer: Nancy Sabato
Photo research by Connie Gardner

Cover image by Aimee Vance
The photographs in this book are used by permission and through the courtesy of:
Getty Images: AFP, 1, 9, 48, 55, 66, 75, 79, 81, 84; Daniel Berehulak, 4; Tim Graham, 17; De Agostini, 20;
Keystone Stringer, 23; Hulton Archive, 28; Popperfoto, 45; Lichtfield Archive, 72; The Image Works; Topham, 9;
Steve Rubin, 62; AP Photo; 32, 42.

Printed in Malaysia (T)
135642

CONTENTS

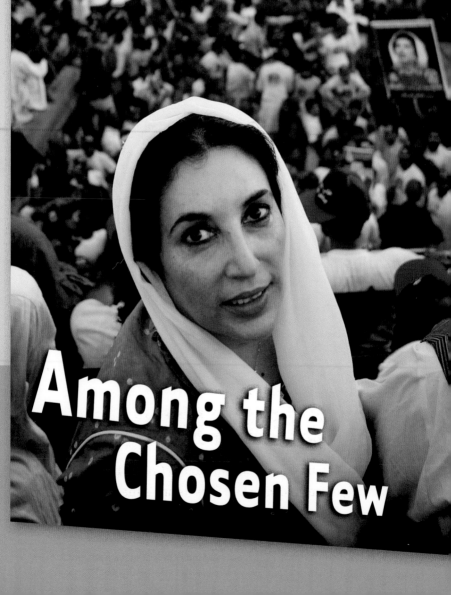

CHAPTER ONE

Among the Chosen Few

I T IS DECEMBER 2, 1988. IN THE CAPITAL CITY of Islamabad near the foot of the Himalayas, an unusual event is taking place. Under a canopy of bright lights, a woman walks slowly down the red carpet in the Presidential Palace. She is wearing the green and white colors of her country's flag. Her name is Benazir Bhutto. She is about to become the prime minister of Pakistan.

It was indeed an unusual event for Benazir Bhutto and for her nation. Pakistan is an Islamic country that lies in the northwest part of the Indian subcontinent. Many of its citizens are poor, but Benazir was born into a prominent and wealthy family. That accident of birth opened the doors to privilege and education, to the world of politics, and, finally, to her assassination.

Benazir was born in Karachi, Pakistan, on June 21, 1953. In 1988 she was sworn in as the first female prime minister of her country. At the age of thirty-five, she became the first woman and the youngest person ever to head the government of a Muslim nation.

Benazir's rise in politics was mainly due to her lineage— that is, her family's position and power. But to appreciate the full significance of her election, it is also important to know something about the religion of Islam.

THE ISLAMIC RELIGION

The word *Islam* means "submission to God." The followers of the religion are known as Muslims. Islam is the second-largest

After eight years of self-imposed exile, Benazir is greeted by thousands as she returns to Karachi in October 2007 to lead her party into national elections.

world religion after Christianity, and it has about one billion believers. The Qur'an (or Koran) is the holy book of their faith. Muslims believe that Allah (God) revealed the verses of the Qur'an to Muhammad, the prophet. The Qur'an provides spiritual and practical guidelines by which Muslims conduct their lives.

Islam is the main religion in Africa, the Middle East, and major parts of Asia. There are also large Muslim communities in Eastern and Western Europe. *The New York Times Almanac 2009* estimates the Muslim population in the United States between 1 and 2 million; however, other estimates put the number as high as 7 million.

Most Muslims belong to one of two denominations: Sunni (SOO-nee; about 85 percent) or Shiite (SHEE-ite; about 15 percent). All Muslims are expected to observe the Five Pillars of Islam, which are the ritual duties upon which a Muslim's life is built. The first pillar is *Shahadah*, the basic creed of Islam and a testimony of faith. *Salat* is the ritual prayer, performed five times a day. *Zakat*, which literally means "growth," is the duty to give to the poor. *Sawm* is the practice of fasting through the month of Ramadan (the ninth month of the Islamic calendar). The word *Ramadan* means "burning or scorching," and in this case it refers to the intense heating sensation in the stomach due to thirst. Others say that Ramadan means a scorching out of sins. During this month, Muslims refrain from eating, drinking, or having sex from dawn to dusk.

As the last pillar, every able-bodied Muslim is called to make at least one pilgrimage to the city of Mecca during his or her lifetime. This pilgrimage is known as the Hajj.

A Muslim place of worship is called a mosque; its Arabic name is *masjid*, which means "a place to prostrate oneself in front of God." Historically, the mosque has also been a site of community and social

MUHAMMAD THE PROPHET

Muhammad ibn Abdullah was born in Mecca (in modern-day Saudi Arabia) in about the year 570. Muslims believe he is the messenger and prophet of God. As a young man, Muhammad retreated to a cave in the mountains to meditate. There, according to Islamic beliefs, he began to receive revelations from God at the age of forty. These revelations form the verses of the Qur'an. Three years later, Muhammad began his public preaching. He told people to surrender to the will of God.

To escape persecution from hostile tribes, Muhammad migrated to Medina in 622. That date became the first year in the Islamic calendar, which is called Hijra (also spelled Hegira). When Muhammad died in 632, most of the Arabian Peninsula had been converted to Islam.

interaction and Islamic learning. A mosque usually has a minaret, which is a tall, slender tower from which followers are called to worship. Unlike a Catholic church or a synagogue, a mosque does not have furniture. Worshipers prostrate themselves on the floor in the direction of the Kaaba in Mecca, the most holy shrine for people of Islam.

There is a complex relationship between Islam and women in Muslim societies. Traditionally, as in many other countries and cultures, Muslims have preferred the birth of boys more than that of girls because boys represent continuance of the family line and future wages. There are also complex laws regarding the right of inheritance. In some Muslim cultures, a woman's inheritance may be smaller than a man's because the male is held responsible for his family, which includes his parents and sisters. Today, Muslim women work in many occupations; in Pakistan, for instance, there is a growing number of female doctors, especially in rural areas.

In general, Islam prescribes modest dress in public for both men and women. In practice, however, the dress code has been more restrictive for women. Some Muslim women wear the burqa, or burka. This garment covers a woman from head to toe, sometimes just leaving slits for her eyes. Today, a Muslim woman's use of the burqa has to do with her particular culture and social class. The garment is more traditional in Afghanistan or rural parts of Pakistan, for instance, than in the rest of Pakistan or in other Muslim nations. In Pakistan's urban areas, many women cut their hair short and regard the burqa as old-fashioned. Others might stay with tradition. Benazir Bhutto, although not regarded as traditional, always wore a head covering in public.

The seclusion of women from men or other strangers in Islamic countries is known as purdah. This may include the concealing burqa as well as seclusion in a family compound. Women may spend much of their lives enclosed within the family compound walls. When a woman marries, she may enter the compound of her husband's family. In strict practice, women are allowed to leave the compound perhaps once a week to visit their families. Such rules are not prevalent today, although purdah is practiced to some degree in many Muslim nations.

In recent years, Islamic leaders have fought for more equal treatment between the sexes. There have been some changes. Aside from Brunei and Saudi Arabia (where only men can vote), women can now vote in all Muslim-majority nations.

Showing identification cards, Afghan women clad in the traditional burqa cast their votes.

In Lebanon, however, a woman must provide proof of education in order to vote; there is no such requirement for men.

As a woman of Pakistan born into wealthy circumstances in the mid-twentieth century, Benazir Bhutto might have led a comfortable, uneventful life. But her parents' ideas about education and culture opened up a different path.

GROWING UP NON-TRADITIONALLY

Benazir Bhutto was the first of four children born to Begum Nusrat and Zulfikar Ali Bhutto. Her name means "without equal," but her father called her Pinkie because she had rosy cheeks. In many families all over the world, the first child holds a special place. That was certainly true for the Bhuttos. Benazir's father was extremely fond of his firstborn child, and he showed it. She grew up happy, loved, and pampered.

The Bhuttos were one of the land-rich families in Pakistan. They lived in a huge home on the outskirts of Karachi, which is the capital of Sindh province on the Arabian Sea. The Bhutto home had a staff of about twenty-one servants to care for the family's needs.

Where did the Bhuttos' wealth come from? For centuries, a good deal of the farmland in Sindh province belonged to members of the Bhutto family. In Pakistan, as in most agricultural countries, land is equivalent to wealth. Benazir remembered this story from her childhood: The British conqueror of Sindh, Charles Napier, was touring the province in 1843. He asked who owned the land and was told it belonged to the Bhuttos. "Wake me up when we are off Bhutto's lands," Napier said. But when he woke up later on his own, he was still on Bhutto land. Benazir said her father loved telling that story.

Benazir's grandfather, Shah Nawaz Bhutto, was born in the Sindh province of British India, now part of Pakistan, and went to school in Great Britain. He was knighted for his work when the British occupied Pakistan. Land given to him by the British made him a wealthy and influential landowner. He began to break the practice of requiring Bhuttos to marry only other Bhuttos—first or second cousins. This so-called arranged marriage—an ancient practice in many civilizations—kept Bhutto land within the family. In fact, there was such a contract between Benazir's father and his cousin Amir. They were twelve and nine years old at the time. They did not actually live together. She stayed in her family home, and he eventually went to the University of California in the United States. Then he studied law at Oxford University in England before returning to Pakistan.

Despite this traditional arranged marriage, Nawaz Bhutto shocked the other Pakistani landowners because he educated his daughters as well as his sons. He even sent the girls to school! Not only was it unusual to educate daughters, but many of the landowners did not even educate their sons. They reasoned that both sons and daughters would always have land and therefore would always have a more than comfortable livelihood. Education seemed unnecessary.

Benazir's mother was also probably a bit of a shock to the other landowners. For one thing, she was college educated. Nusrat was the daughter of a wealthy Iranian businessman. She was far more cosmopolitan than even the progressive women of the extended Bhutto family, who still lived largely within the walls of their compounds. But Nusrat and her sisters rode around town in their own cars and did not wear traditional veils. Zulfikar and Nusrat were married in 1951. After Benazir's birth, her brother Mir Murtaza was born in 1954, her sister Sanam (called Sunny) in 1957, and another brother, Shah Nawaz, a year later. From the time that Benazir was old enough to understand anything, she understood that she and her sister would be educated just like her two brothers. Her father was determined to treat his sons and daughters equally. Benazir also understood at a young age that she would be the first woman in the Bhutto family to study abroad as her father had done.

Benazir was enrolled in the Lady Jennings Nursery School in

Karachi at the age of three. At age five, she went to the Convent of Jesus and Mary, also in Karachi. Irish nuns ran the convent. School hours ran from 7:45 a.m. until 1:15 p.m., with a tea break at 10:30. In the afternoons after school, Benazir and her siblings had private tutors to instruct them in English and math. The Bhutto children were always taught in English, which was the language mainly spoken in the household. Benazir also learned Urdu, the national language of Pakistan. In addition, her father spoke Sindhi, the language of his province, and her mother, being Iranian, spoke Farsi.

In her first years of school, Benazir wore a simple white dress to class. In high school, she wore a *shalwar* and *kameez*, which are Urdu terms for baggy pants and a tunic-like shirt. They were white with a long, green scarf—a *dupatta*—that crossed from the shoulder to the waist. Besides her regular schoolwork, Benazir studied Islam.

When Benazir was about nine years old, her mother, a Shiite Muslim, attempted to raise her daughter in the old ways of Islam. During a train ride to Larkana, Nusrat draped Benazir in a black burqa. Benazir later wrote that entering the world of adults was a disappointment. The black cloth blurred her eyesight, and its length made it difficult to walk. However, when Nusrat later told Benazir's father that his oldest daughter had worn the burqa, he replied that there was no need for her to wear it. He said,

Let her be judged by her character and her mind, not by her clothing.

And so, according to Benazir, "I became the first Bhutto woman to be released from a life spent in perpetual twilight."

Benazir was relieved that she did not have to wear the burqa. She was even more relieved when she heard another of her father's decisions. He spoke to her mother about the practice of keeping Bhutto marriages within the family. Her father declared,

I don't want the boys to marry their cousins and leave them behind our compound walls any more than I want my daughters buried alive behind some other relative's compound walls. . . . Let them finish their education first. Then they can decide what to do with their lives.

In her autobiography, *Daughter of Destiny*, Benazir said her father's decision meant that he was determined to bring his children into the twentieth century.

GROWING UP PAKISTANI

In Urdu, *Pakistan* means "land of the pure." It is also a land of great physical beauty. It has seven of the sixteen tallest mountain peaks in Asia. The tallest is K2 in the Karakoram Range of the Himalayas. At 28,251 feet (8,611 m), K2 is the world's second-highest mountain; only Everest, also in the Himalayas, is taller, at 29,035 feet (8,850 m). Pakistan is bordered by India to the east, Afghanistan and Iran to the west, Afghanistan and China to the north, and the Arabian Sea to the south.

THE SAVAGE MOUNTAIN

Mount Everest may be the tallest mountain in the world, but K2 is arguably the most difficult mountain to climb. The routes to the summit are harder to scale than those on Everest, and the weather on K2 is less predictable and much colder. It is said that for every four climbers who get to the summit, one dies trying.

After many failed attempts, two Italians named Lino Lacedelli and Achille Compagnoni finally reached the top of K2 in 1954. Since that time, the mountain has been climbed successfully 189 times, compared with about 1,400 times for Everest. K2 is known as the savage mountain because it is so treacherous to climb. The peak was thought to be especially deadly for women climbers. The first woman reached the summit of K2 in 1986, but the next four female climbers died in the attempt. However, in August 2008, Mi-Sun Go became the eleventh woman to scale the savage mountain.

Pakistan covers an area of about 310,320 square miles (803,725 square km), making it nearly twice the size of California. According to *The New York Times Almanac 2009*, it is the world's sixth-largest country in terms of population, following China, India, the United States, Indonesia, and Brazil. About 176 million people live in its four provinces: Balochistan, Sindh, the Punjab, and the North-West Frontier.

Balochistan is the largest province but has few people—only about 4 percent of the national total—because of the inhospitable Makran desert. Its capital and biggest city is Quetta. The largest city in the Sindh province is Karachi—the original capital and Benazir's birthplace—on the Arabian Sea. The country's only seaport, Karachi has a population of about 18 million. The densely populated Punjab province contains Islamabad, Pakistan's capital since the 1970s, as well as Lahore, the country's second-largest city and its cultural center. The North-West Frontier Province, usually called NWFP, borders Afghanistan. Its capital city is Peshawar. This area contains many tribal peoples who are outside the control of the national government. The largest group is the Pashtuns, who through the years, have called for independence from Pakistan.

Today, Pakistan's most pressing problems are illiteracy, poverty, and lack of economic opportunity. Wherever these problems appear worldwide, they are fertile grounds for intolerance and discrimination. According to a 2008 report by UNESCO, close to 50 percent of Pakistanis cannot read. Only about 60 percent of the children attend ten years of school, and only 12 percent attend twelve years. Millions of Pakistan's people, especially those in rural areas, are classified as poor.

Pakistan is a complex land and a complex mixture of peoples. Aryans, Persians, Greeks, and Mongols have left their mark through the centuries. So has British rule. Pakistan is an Islamic state, which also heavily influences its past, present, and future. The country came into being in an effort to protect the rights of Muslims living in India.

ANCIENT PAKISTAN

The land that shaped the life and destiny of Benazir Bhutto has two histories: the Pakistan of long ago and the nation that gained independence in 1947.

Relics of Stone Age humans have been found in Pakistan's Soan Valley near Rawalpindi in the north. They date to 500,000 BCE.

In 1974, the site of Mehrgarh was discovered on the Kachi plain in Balochistan. These people—who lived between 7000 and 2600 BCE—built mud brick houses and used tools made of copper ore. They herded sheep and cattle and grew barley and wheat.

As the plain became more arid, civilization moved on to the Indus Valley, where it flourished about 2500 BCE. At its peak, about 5 million people occupied hundreds of settlements extending to the Arabian Sea and the Himalayas. But the civilization ended abruptly. The probable causes were a devastating earthquake and the appearance of the Aryans, who began to migrate into the region. Buddhist writings of the fifth and sixth centuries BCE mention the state of Gandhara in the Indus Valley. Alexander the Great conquered much of the Punjab region around 334 BCE.

Over the next centuries, different peoples flooded the area. Muslim Arabs established deep roots during the seventh century CE. The warlord Tamerlane ransacked the northern regions in 1398. During the early 1500s, Mogul warriors invaded and remained.

It was not until the eighteenth century that the first European traders arrived in the region. The most important of these was the British East India Company, which became the Mogul Empire's main trading partner. Because the company had the backing of the British military, the Mogul emperor authorized it to collect taxes. That led to the idea of turning the area into a British colony. In 1784, Great Britain passed the India Act, which put the British East India Company under government control. By 1818 the company—and therefore Great Britain—had nearly complete rule of the region that would become India and Pakistan. In 1843 the British took over the Sindh province, followed by the Punjab in 1849. But the northern tribes refused to be conquered, so the British gave up and created the North-West Frontier, over which it had little control.

A mural of Tamerlane, or Timur the Great, who conquered much of western and central Asia in the fourteenth century

THE NEW NATION

As the twentieth century neared, Hindus and Muslims in the new colony became more and more dissatisfied with British rule. In 1857, the sepoys (Indian natives who worked as soldiers for the British East India Company) staged a mutiny. Although they had many grievances, the final spark for the mutiny was the new Enfield rifle. To load the rifle, a sepoy had to bite open the cartridge, which was covered with pork fat (forbidden to Muslims) or beef fat (which Hindus do not eat).

The sepoy mutiny inspired the idea of an independent nation. The Indian National Congress (INC) was created in 1885 with the aim of eventual independence. At the outset, the INC included the interests of both religions—Hinduism and Islam. But the Hindus far outnumbered the Muslims, who began to fear that an independent India would not have their interests at heart. They were especially disturbed in 1900, when the British allowed Hindi to become the official language of the area. That led to the creation of the All-India Muslim League in 1906. The league did not yet seek an independent Muslim state, but it concentrated on protecting Muslim liberties and rights.

Mohammad Ali Jinnah, known as the father of Pakistan, joined the All-India Muslim League in 1913, after it began to call for Indian independence. Jinnah was convinced at this point that cooperation between Muslims and Hindus would lead to an independent, united India. He became the league's president in 1916 and negotiated the Lucknow Pact with the INC. This brought the two parties together on most issues. But he broke with the INC in 1920 when its leader, Mohandas Gandhi, launched a law that violated the Non-Cooperation Movement against the British. Jinnah also became convinced that the INC would renounce support for separate electorates for Muslims, which it would do in 1928.

After World War I, Great Britain began to work toward creating an independent India. But the All-India Muslim League refused to participate in any discussion that did not include an independent Muslim state. In 1933, Rahmat Ali, a law student at Cambridge University in England, wrote a pamphlet entitled "Now or Never." In it he coined the name Pakistan, taking letters from names of the provinces he thought should form the new Muslim country.

In 1946, the British tried one last time to create a single country by proposing a plan for the new Dominion of India. But an alternative plan was proposed to divide the land into a Hindu-majority India and a Muslim-majority Pakistan. The INC rejected the alternative plan,

Mohammad Ali Jinnah (c.1945), Indian politician known as the father of Pakistan

and the All-India Muslim League planned a general strike on August 16 to protest the rejection. This nearly resulted in war between Hindus and Muslims. In the massive riots that followed in the city of Calcutta, more than 4,000 people died, and 100,000 were left homeless. At this point the partition of India seemed inevitable, so the British reluctantly agreed to the two-nation concept.

At midnight on August 14, 1947, the newly independent nations of Pakistan and India joined the British Commonwealth. But the seeds of trouble had already been sown. The trouble soon would involve Benazir Bhutto and her family.

CHAPTER TWO

In the Land
of the Pure

WHILE BENAZIR WAS GROWING UP IN A world of books and tutors, she was also growing up in a world of politics. Her father was an educated man with degrees from both the University of California and Oxford. Although he took over management of the family business, his main interest was his country. In 1957, when Benazir was just four years old, Zulfikar Ali Bhutto became the youngest member of the Pakistani delegation to the United Nations.

For the first several years of independence, Pakistan was ruled by General Muhammad Ayub Khan and his strong military. In 1962, Khan appointed Bhutto to the post of foreign minister. During Benazir's young years, her father was away from home much of the time. Since her mother generally traveled with Zulfikar, the household staff often took care of the Bhutto children.

In 1963, when Benazir was ten years old, she was sent to the Convent of Jesus and Mary boarding school in Murree along with Sunny, who was then seven. Life was different for the Bhutto girls during their two years at Murree. For one thing, they had to make their own beds and shine their own shoes. For another, the school had no central heating system, so it was quite cold during the winter months. Benazir and Sunny slept in dorms with about twenty other girls. Their father told the nuns that his daughters were to be treated like any other student. Even from a distance, he was never out of touch with their education. By letter or telephone, he had reports on their progress. When they

Called the savage mountain, K2 is the world's second-highest peak, topped only by Mount Everest.

were at home and he returned from a foreign trip, he asked for first-hand accounts of their studies.

Sometimes, when Benazir had time off from school, she traveled with her father. She remembered an incident in his private railroad car in late 1963. Bhutto woke his daughter to tell her that the young president of the United States, John F. Kennedy, had been assassinated. She also remembered meeting important government leaders who traveled to Pakistan, such as Chou En-lai, the premier of China, and U.S. vice president Hubert Humphrey. Benazir recalled that she mistook Humphrey for comedian Bob Hope, whom she had seen in a movie.

A GOVERNMENT IN TURMOIL

Ink had hardly dried on the documents that created India and Pakistan when trouble started. When the British set the nations' boundaries, they divided Pakistan into two parts, separated by India. The reason for this unusual arrangement was that the heavily populated Muslim areas were on opposite ends of the subcontinent, 1,000 miles (1,600 kilometers) apart. So, the new country was divided from the start; the northeastern area was named East Pakistan, and the northwestern region was called West Pakistan.

The separation was a disaster for two reasons. To get from the eastern to the western parts of Pakistan meant crossing through a foreign country—India. In addition, the Bengali people who dominated the east region were much different in language and culture from those in the west, even though they were all Muslims. The Bengalis feared that the west, which held the real political power, would not protect their interests. They were even more convinced when Urdu was declared the only state language of Pakistan. Most of East Pakistan spoke Bengali. Almost immediately, the Bengalis began to press for independence. Leaders in West Pakistan, however, including Benazir's father, seemed determined to hang on to power at whatever cost.

To add to the problem, Pakistan now faced a fight with India. Left unsettled by the British was the question of which nation got the state of Jammu and Kashmir. (In Pakistan the area is referred to as Indian-occupied Kashmir.) The population of Jammu and Kashmir was mainly Muslim, but the leader was Hindu. In September 1965 Pakistan, at the urging of Zulfikar Ali Bhutto, sent troops into Jammu and Kashmir in what was known as Operation Grand Slam. In response, India dispatched its troops, which enraged Pakistani leaders. Suddenly, in October, there was war. This was the first of three India-Pakistan fights over Jammu and Kashmir. (The two countries would fight again in 1971 and 1999. Today, India controls about 60 percent of Jammu

A Pakistani village was almost totally destroyed by raiders in 1965.

JAMMU AND KASHMIR: THE DISPUTED LAND

For a small region about the size of Utah, Jammu and Kashmir has long been the site of a large dispute. It covers some 85,000 square miles (220,000 sq km) of the subcontinent of India. Only about 5 percent of this mountainous land can be farmed. Even so, agriculture is its main source of income. However, its breathtaking mountain scenery attracts many tourists each year. The Indian-held part of the region in the south and east has most of the fertile land and most of the population, which numbers some 10 million people.

and Kashmir, Pakistan has 30 percent, and China has occupied 10 percent since 1962.)

In the midst of fierce fighting, Zulfikar Ali Bhutto delivered a fiery speech at the UN Security Council in New York City. He condemned India for its actions and declared,

We will fight for a thousand years.

But after about two weeks, both India and Pakistan yielded to strong political pressure from the United States, Great Britain, and the Soviet Union. The United Nations stepped in to stop the fighting. Zulfikar Ali Bhutto and Ayub Khan drew up a peace treaty calling for troops to withdraw to prewar boundaries. That move turned out to be very unpopular in Pakistan, and later, Bhutto himself criticized the final treaty. Because of his growing disagreement with Khan, Bhutto resigned his post in June 1967. He traveled the country and delivered political speeches. This was his message:

"Islam is our faith, democracy is our policy, socialism is our economy. All power to the people.""

In November, he founded the Pakistan Peoples Party (PPP) in Lahore. The first floor of the Bhutto home in Karachi was turned into a PPP office to spread Zulfikar's pro-democracy program across the country.

A SURGE OF VIOLENCE

This was an unsettled time for Benazir and her siblings. Tension between her father and supporters of Ayub Khan grew thicker. Threats and charges of corruption against the government grew louder. Demonstrations and riots broke out across the country. Finally, in 1968, Khan arrested Bhutto and threw him in jail. He was taken to a prison in Mianwali and then was transferred to Sahiwal, where he was put into solitary confinement. Benazir received a letter from him late in the year. He told her how proud he was that she was going to take the O-level exams at the young age of fifteen. These exams were critical for her possible entrance into Radcliffe College at Harvard University in the United States. While her father was in prison and the rest of the family was in Lahore, Benazir remained at their home in Karachi and studied.

The exams were given once a year in December. Benazir took

them at the Vatican Embassy in Clifton, a wealthy neighborhood in Karachi. School officials thought she would be safe there, as riots grew fiercer all over the city and country. She did indeed pass the O-levels at age fifteen and then went on to Karachi Grammar School.

As the riots continued, there were calls for Ayub Khan to resign and to release the political prisoners. About three months after his arrest, Bhutto was set free. He was sent by train to Larkana, where Benazir and her family met him. She said later that she never forgot his arrival because a Khan supporter tried to shoot him as he stepped off the train. The gun misfired, but the crowd—PPP supporters— grabbed the young shooter and began to beat him. Her father warned her not to look.

With the country seemingly about to descend into total chaos, Ayub Khan resigned in March 1969. According to the constitution, the next in line was speaker of the National Assembly of Pakistan. Instead, Ayub Khan designated Yahya Khan, another military man, as Pakistan's new leader. His first act was to suspend all civil law.

OFF TO AMERICA

Amid the chaos, Benazir received a letter in April. It said she had been accepted to enter Radcliffe College in the fall. At the age of sixteen, she would be among the youngest of its students. For all her impressive schoolwork and life of relative luxury, Benazir was a shy young woman who knew little about the world. Even the college officials cautioned her father against sending her there at such an early age. But he felt she would do well. Bhutto gave his daughter a leather-bound copy of the Qur'an and told her to study hard.

Nusrat flew to Massachusetts with Benazir before the September term in 1969 and stayed for two weeks. Initially, it was difficult for the young girl to adjust to being around so many strangers. For the first time in her life, she was among people who did not know that she was the daughter of a wealthy and prominent family in her country. In fact, many of the young women of Radcliffe at the time were unaware that there was such a nation as Pakistan. In her autobiography, Bhutto writes of adjusting to life in college:

> I was attentive to her [Nusrat's] directions for prayer, but not to her wardrobe [a warm woolen garment] which was impractical in the rain and snow and set me apart from the other students. I . . . re-emerged in jeans and sweatshirts from the Harvard Co-op. I let my hair grow long and straight and was flattered when my friends in Eliot Hall told me I looked like Joan Baez.

Gradually, Benazir made friends, and her shyness subsided. There was so much going on, such as nationwide protests against the war in Vietnam. Benazir joined thousands of American college students who marched on Boston Common and in Washington, D.C., to protest the continuing conflict. At the Washington rally, she had her first experience with tear gas.

At Radcliffe, Benazir befriended John Kenneth Galbraith and his family. Galbraith was an economics professor at Harvard and had been ambassador to India. Benazir's father had written to Galbraith and asked him to keep an eye on his daughter. She often

Pakistan's future prime minister as a college student in the United States, 1972

went to the Galbraith home and considered them a second family.

It was also an exciting time to be at Harvard because the women's movement was spreading in the United States. At late-night meetings, young women gathered and talked about what they would do with their lives now that the future seemed endless. As Benazir felt more at home expressing her views, she became more relaxed among her friends. She even became the social secretary at Eliot Hall and gave guided tours of the campus.

THE NEVER-ENDING CONFLICT

The Vietnam War was fought in Vietnam, Laos, and Cambodia from 1959 until April 30, 1975. The government of South Vietnam, supported by the United States and other countries, opposed the communist government of North Vietnam and its communist allies. U.S. involvement was intended to prevent a communist takeover of South Vietnam. It was part of a plan called containment. But as the years passed, American involvement grew deeper, and Americans became increasingly divided over escalating deaths and the financial costs of war. Finally, in 1975, the forces of North Vietnam were victorious. North and South Vietnam were reunified the next year.

An estimated 4 million Vietnamese on both sides died during the war years, as well as 2 million Laotians and Cambodians. The United States lost more than 58,000 soldiers.

GOOD-BYE TO EAST PAKISTAN AND RADCLIFFE

At Radcliffe Benazir decided to major in comparative government. Her father was delighted. She also listened for reports of what was happening to her own government back home. Like his predecessor, Yahya Khan had little success in fixing domestic problems. So, while no one seemed to be watching, East Pakistan's demand for independence grew stronger.

The Bengalis formed the Awami League, which called for strikes and other forms of civil disobedience. In December 1970 Pakistan held its first elections in thirteen years. The PPP won a large number of seats in West Pakistan, while the Awami League won a majority in the east. Zulfikar Ali Bhutto himself refused to accept the Awami League government. In his book on Pakistan, Owen Bennett Jones describes the disagreement over East Pakistan: "In the year 1971 the future of East Pakistan depended on a struggle between three men: a habitual drunk, General Yahya Kahn; a professional agitator, Sheikh Mujibur Rahman; and a political operator par excellence, Zulfikar Ali Bhutto."

Finally, Yahya Khan sent troops into Dhaka, the capital city of East Pakistan, in March 1971. He outlawed the Awami League and imprisoned its leader, Sheikh Rahman. Benazir remembered how shocked she was at the news. She was even more shocked at the way her fellow students condemned her country for its actions. At first Benazir herself could not believe that Pakistanis could fight each other in such a way.

In early December, a week after the invasion of Dhaka, Bhutto spoke at the United Nations in New York City. He called for a cease-fire. Benazir went to New York and sat in the council room as her father urged that UN forces be sent into the area.

But now the Indian government, led by Indira Gandhi, decided to support East Pakistan's call for independence. That led to the 1971 war between the two countries. Indian forces were victorious on December 16, and East Pakistan became a separate nation. It took the name of Bangladesh, which means "home of the Bengalis." West Pakistan now became simply Pakistan.

General Yahya Khan was forced to resign. With the end of the war, civilians finally took over the government of Pakistan. The new leader was Zulfikar Ali Bhutto, head of the PPP and father of Benazir. He was named president, army commander in chief, and the first civilian chief martial law administrator.

NOTABLE GRADUATES OF RADCLIFFE

When Benazir graduated from college with honors, her diploma read Harvard-Radcliffe. After women tried unsuccessfully to get into Harvard University, Radcliffe was founded in 1879 as Harvard Annex. Harvard faculty taught the classes. The first joint Harvard-Radcliffe diplomas were issued in 1963. A formal merger agreement was signed with Harvard in 1977, and the two schools were merged fully in 1999. Today, the Radcliffe campus in Cambridge, Massachusetts, functions as a research institute within Harvard.

Besides Benazir Bhutto, notable graduates of Radcliffe include authors Gertrude Stein and Helen Keller, astronomer Henrietta Swan Leavitt, and actress Stockard Channing. Bhutto later recalled her years at Radcliffe as among the happiest times of her life. When she was prime minister, she arranged for a gift from her government to Harvard Law School.

In June 1973, Benazir graduated from Radcliffe College at Harvard. Not yet twenty years old, she was quite different from the timid girl who had entered those halls four years earlier. She had made several good friends, and she knew her way around the cities of Cambridge and Boston. Although she was accepted to continue her education at Oxford University in England, she was reluctant to leave the comfort of Cambridge. She asked her father to let her go to law school at Tufts University in Medford, Massachusetts, instead. But he refused; Bhutto knew that his daughter must eventually return to Pakistan. He did not want Benazir to become too used to life in the United States. Benazir said good-bye to Radcliffe and moved on.

A Father's Legacy

W HEN BENAZIR BHUTTO LEFT RADCLIFFE College in June 1973, she did not go immediately to Oxford University. Instead, with her mother and brother she returned to Pakistan to attend the August 14 ceremony during which the National Assembly adopted a new constitution with a charter recognizing Pakistan as an Islamic state. As leader of the majority in the National Assembly, Zulfikar Ali Bhutto was now prime minister.

After Bhutto was named president on December 20, 1971, he appointed a new cabinet and nationalized all the major industries. He increased workers' rights and the power of labor unions. He rescinded martial law and told Pakistani leaders to write a new constitution. In his first address to the country via radio and television, he declared, "We are facing the worst crisis in our country's life, a deadly crisis . . . we will make a new Pakistan, a prosperous and progressive Pakistan."

But for all his intentions, Bhutto did not have an easy time over the next two years. He negotiated a peace treaty with India and secured the release of 93,000 Pakistani prisoners of war. But many Pakistanis thought he made too many concessions to India. By January 1973 he had to send in troops to put down riots in Balochistan, where he dismissed the government. By March, a number of military officers were arrested for plotting against him. However, on April 12, he signed a new constitution that established Pakistan as an Islamic republic. In July,

Benazir (*extreme left*) attends a meeting in India between her father, Ali Bhutto (*second from left*), and Indian prime minister Indira Gandhi (*right*), July 3, 1972.

he officially recognized the nation of Bangladesh. On August 10, he turned over the position of president to Fazal Ilahi Chaudhry in order to become prime minister.

Benazir and her family watched from the prime minister's box on August 14 as the people of Pakistan were given their first constitution that protected human rights. It separated executive and judicial branches of government. During its four years of legal operation, the constitution outlawed discrimination based on sex, race, or religion.

LIFE AT OXFORD

In fall 1973, Benazir left Pakistan to enter Oxford University in England, some twenty-two years after her father. So far she had lived a relatively anonymous life of ease and comfort, but the reality of her public station in life was only a reminder away. Benazir's father sent her just such a reminder in a letter he wrote to his daughter soon after her arrival:

Here I see your presence like mine in flesh and blood, over every cobble of the streets of Oxford, over every step you take on the frozen stone ladders, through every portal of learning you enter. Your being at Oxford is a dream come true. We pray and hope that this dream turned into reality will grow into a magnificent career in the service of your people.

OXFORD, THE CENTER OF LEARNING

Oxford University is one of the world's great historic centers of learning. Located on the Thames River about 50 miles (80.5 km) northwest of London, Oxford has been a university since 1167. (It did not become coeducational for another 792 years!) Oxford is most famous for its individualized instruction called tutorials. For a bachelor's degree, a student must study for three years. Some of England's—and the world's—most prominent people have attended Oxford. They include a number of British prime ministers, as well as Benazir Bhutto and her father.

At first, however, Oxford did not seem so magnificent to Benazir. Unlike her father, who loved his stay there, she found the English students very reserved and her living quarters rather sparse after Radcliffe. She also missed having her own telephone. But her father kept reminding her of the reason she was at Oxford. He even sent her a print of ancient Rome that he had hung on his wall when he was there. Benazir put it on her wall as well.

Benazir also took her father's advice and joined the Oxford Union Debating Society. Since 1823 this society has been valuable training ground for stepping into political life. The Oxford Union, as it is commonly known, has a reputation for the cut and thrust of its debates. Its members are mostly, but not entirely, from Oxford University. The Oxford Union is an independent society.

Benazir did not join the debating society as a door opener for politics. At the time, she had no interest in a political career. As she later said, she had seen the strain that politics creates for so many people. Instead, she joined the Oxford Union to please her father. And in so doing, she found it to be one of the best experiences of her time in England. In fact, in December 1976, she was named president of the society, the first Asian woman in that position. During her time as president, she organized four serious debates and an amusing final one. It had a rock and roll theme and was titled "This House Likes Dominating Women." She also gained valuable experience that would serve her well when, as prime minister, she had to speak before thousands of Pakistanis.

Interestingly, Benazir's first speech in the main debating chamber concerned whether U.S. president Richard M. Nixon should be removed from office. Nixon, the thirty-seventh American president (in office 1968-1974), became involved in the June 1972 Watergate scandal. Before his run for reelection, five men were arrested for breaking and entering the Democratic National Committee headquarters in Washington, D.C. Nixon was reelected handily that fall. But his involvement in Watergate finally forced him to resign from office or face impeachment. In August 1974 he became the first U.S. president to resign. After the debate at Oxford, according to Benazir,

The motion to impeach President Nixon was carried by a vote of 345 to 2. . . . Guns, not votes, would overthrow my father in Pakistan.

Benazir at Oxford University, November 1976

TROUBLE AT HOME

As Benazir was starting a new life at Oxford, her father was starting a new life as prime minister of Pakistan. Neither adjustment was easy.

Pakistan was created as an Islamic republic with a parliamentary form of government. Great Britain has a parliamentary government, as do Canada and Russia. In the United States, which is a federal republic, one person—the president—is both the head of government and the head of state. In a parliamentary system, there is usually a clear difference between the two positions. The head of state is often a figurehead, called the president and elected by the people or by the parliament. In Great Britain, the monarch, Queen Elizabeth II, is the ceremonial head of state, but the prime minister runs the country.

The prime minister, or premier, usually holds the power in a parliamentary system. He or she may be a member of parliament. In some systems, the prime minister can select and dismiss other members of the cabinet. In Pakistan, the prime minister is elected by the National Assembly, which in turn is elected by popular vote. The leader of the party that has the most votes in the National Assembly becomes prime minister. However, the president of Pakistan has the right to remove the prime minister and impose new elections.

The office of prime minister of Pakistan was created when the nation was created in 1947. Over the next few years, the heads of state removed a number of prime ministers from office. In 1958, the office of prime minister was discontinued, and martial law reigned. But Bhutto's 1973 constitution restored executive power to the office of prime minister.

Over the next four years, Bhutto developed closer relations with other Muslim countries such as Saudi Arabia. He was host to the Second Islamic Summit of Muslim Nations in Lahore in 1974. Benazir flew home that February to be part of the summit. She left with a feeling that it was a great success for the country and for her father. But Benazir also knew that many Pakistanis were criticizing her father on religious and other grounds. For instance, they complained that he refused to declare the Ahmadiyya community to be non-Muslim.

The Ahmadiyya movement follows the teachings of Mirza Ghulam Ahmad of India. Followers declare the movement to be a revitalization of Islam. They claim to practice Islam as taught by Muhammad. Other Muslims disagree. When riots broke out over the issue, Bhutto finally yielded to the pressure. The constitution was changed so that it now defines a Muslim as "a person who believes in the finality of the Prophet Muhammad."

Despite Bhutto's efforts to nationalize the agricultural and consumer industries, Pakistan's economy continued to fail. In 1976, he surprised the country by appointing General Muhammad Zia-ul-Haq as the chief of army staff. He had skipped over five generals who were senior to Zia. This proved to be a mistake.

Internal troubles now plagued the government. An opposition group, the Awami National Party (ANP), was formed. It was banned after one of Bhutto's lieutenants died in a bomb blast. Then internal trouble erupted in the prime minister's own party, the PPP. When a party dissident, Ahmed Raza Kasuri, was murdered, members accused Bhutto of the crime. Early in 1977 the Pakistan National Alliance (PNA) was formed, and it called for new elections. When the election retained the present government, the PNA said it was illegitimate, and the ANP said the process was rigged. Outspoken leaders began to call for the overthrow of the prime minister.

RETURN TO PAKISTAN

While she continued her studies at Oxford, Benazir was well aware of her father's troubles at home. Her family mailed Pakistani newspapers to her, and she listened to radio reports. After she became president of the Oxford Union, she flew home for a winter vacation. At that time, she met General Zia. On such visits, Zulfikar Ali Bhutto confided his feelings about governing to his daughter. He talked to her about the upcoming elections and the changes he hoped would bring stability and peace to Pakistan.

Benazir was busy at Oxford. Besides participating in the debating society, she had to write two or three essays each week and then discuss them with her instructors. In her sparse free time, she drove around Oxford in the yellow car that was her family's graduation present from Harvard. She also made trips to London and went to Stratford-on-Avon for a Shakespeare play. It was a full and exciting life for a young woman.

The three years passed quickly. When they ended, at her father's insistence, she returned to Oxford in 1976 for one more year to study international law. This time, she was not alone. Her brother Mir was now a first-year student at Oxford.

Finally, all the studies were over. During her time at Oxford, Benazir had changed her ideas about her life's work. Now twenty-four years old, she returned to her homeland to begin what she hoped would be a diplomatic career. Little did she realize the turmoil and danger she and her famous family were about to face. On June 25, 1977, she and Mir joined their parents at the prime minister's residence in Rawalpindi, near the capital city of Islamabad. Sunny came home from Harvard. Shah Nawaz returned from his school in Switzerland. They could not know that this was the last time the Bhutto family would have a joyous celebration together.

THE FALL OF THE HOUSE OF BHUTTO

Over the next few days, Benazir settled in to life back in Pakistan. She also settled in to a job. She began as what could be described as a lowly clerk in her father's office. But any dreams of a bright future seemed to be abruptly shattered early in the morning of July 5, 1977. The entire household at Rawalpindi was awakened by the shouts of Benazir's mother telling everyone to get up. The army had taken over! Bhutto's government had suffered a coup d'état. He was overthrown by General Zia. (A coup d'état—pronounced KOO day tah—is a sudden and unconstitutional overthrow of a government by a small group, often the military. The name comes from a French term meaning "a stroke of state.")

Benazir Bhutto's safe and sheltered life was gone in an instant. What would happen to her father and her family? What would happen to her country?

While everyone hurriedly dressed, Benazir's father contacted Zia by telephone. The general protested that he had had no choice but to order the coup in order to keep the country from rioting. However, he gave assurances that new elections would be held in ninety days and that the prime minister would be elected once again. In the meantime, Zulfikar Ali Bhutto would be held in protective custody.

Bhutto believed that Zia was behind the coup, but he told his children there was no point in resisting. To do so might incur great retaliation.

Over the next few hours, Benazir and her family waited for the army to come for her father. Zia said Bhutto would be taken into custody at 2:30 a.m., but by 8:00 a.m. no one had arrived. Benazir waited in agony to find out what would happen to her family. In the meantime, her mother urged her and her siblings to pack. She wanted them out of the country. Just before 9:00 a.m., a black Mercedes arrived in front of the prime minister's home. Without time to say good-bye, Benazir watched her father as he disappeared into the car and it drove away.

Bhutto was taken to Murree, an out-of-the-way location, which the generals may have thought would keep the prime minister's name out of the news. But Bhutto remained popular with the people. His capture meant the end of democracy; Zia suspended the constitution, and martial law now ruled the country. Strict laws took over.

A family photo taken less than a year before Ali Bhutto's death: left, mother Nusrat, brother Shah Nawaz, father Ali Bhutto, Benazir. Foreground left, brother Mir Murtaza, sister Sanam

Previously, if a Muslim broke the rules during the holy month of Ramadan—such as eating or drinking in public during daylight hours—the punishment might only be a look of disapproval. But under Zia, the same act would most likely result in arrest. Zia closed restaurants so that people could not eat in public during Ramadan. He shut off water fountains at the universities so no one could drink. Smoking cigarettes in public was cause for arrest. Fanatic gangs owned the streets at night. Benazir later said she should have realized that her father's arrest was the end of democracy for Pakistan.

But as the days passed, a sense of confidence began to return to the Bhutto family. Zulfikar Ali Bhutto remained very popular with the Pakistani people, as did the PPP. And her father's arrest also put Benazir in the public spotlight. In any country under certain circumstances, it is not unusual for rumors to suddenly take on truth. When many of Pakistan's crops failed that summer, people spread rumors that Bhutto was responsible. From his exile, he urged his daughter to go to Lahore, where the crop failure was profound. Her presence would show the people that the Bhutto family cared for them.

A nervous Benazir and her younger brother Shah Nawaz arrived in Lahore. A large and friendly reception awaited them. It was Benazir's first experience as a political figure. She got over her nervousness when her father telephoned and told her to relay a message speaking of his sorrow at all that had been lost.

The Pakistani people's continued support of the Bhuttos caused Zia's plan to backfire. Three weeks after the coup, Benazir's father was released. The family met him at their home in Karachi, where great crowds gathered to welcome him. Once inside the house, Benazir began to speak of Zia as a coward and a traitor. Her father was quick to silence her; he indicated with his hands that their home was now probably bugged. Although he had been freed, Bhutto realized that he and his family remained in danger. He wanted his younger children to return to school and suggested that Benazir leave the country for a time.

Zia scheduled elections for October 18, and Bhutto was eager to get back into campaigning. But Zia was well aware of the prime minister's popularity. One night in September, five men burst into the Bhutto residence with machine guns. Once more, Benazir's father was taken to jail. The judge could find no evidence for the arrest, however, and he was released.

Despite all the unrest and chaos, the PPP remained popular, and it seemed obvious that the party would win the next election. As head of the party, Bhutto would become prime minister once again. On September 17, he was arrested yet again. This time he was placed in the Karachi Central Jail and then moved to Lahore. In his place, Nusrat Bhutto began to campaign for her husband. Benazir gave speeches as well. Zia responded by placing Benazir under house arrest for fifteen days.

After the house arrest ended, Benazir and her mother went to Lahore for Bhutto's trial. He was charged with the murder of dissident party member Ahmed Raza Kasuri. When PPP members began to organize demonstrations for Bhutto's release, the upcoming elections were cancelled.

On March 18, 1978, Bhutto was found guilty of murder and was sentenced to death. Benazir's mother appealed the verdict, and an appeal was finally granted in December. The following February, the former prime minister was found guilty in a four-to-three majority. The death sentence was upheld. The United States, Great Britain, and Saudi Arabia protested the sentence and asked for clemency. Their requests went unheard. But many in Pakistan and the rest of the world doubted Bhutto's guilt.

Benazir saw her father for the last time on April 3, 1979. He told her how much he loved her. The following morning, the government reported that Zulfikar Ali Bhutto had been hanged.

With heavy hearts and under heavy guard, Nusrat and Benazir visited the unmarked grave of their husband and father. He was laid in the family burial ground in Larkana. Shortly afterward, the two women were allowed to return to their home in Karachi. It was there that Benazir began in earnest to carry on the work of her father. Once more, the house in Karachi became PPP headquarters. At the time,

In November 1979 the Bhutto brothers Shah Nawaz and Mir Murtaza (*second and third from left*) lead a street protest in London against their father's nearing execution.

the Bhutto name still held enough weight for members of the PPP to be satisfied with her as party leader.

JAIL AND EXILE

The PPP may have been satisfied with Benazir, but General Zia was not. Fearing her growing support, he placed her and her mother under house arrest at the Bhutto family home, Al-Murtaza, in the city of Larkana, for six months. Zia wanted the Bhutto name out of the newspapers. Benazir had to deal not only with the boredom of house arrest, but also with a painful ear infection. She worried about becoming deaf. In addition, after hearing that the Soviet army invaded Afghanistan in late 1979, she worried about the safety of her two brothers. After the coup, Mir and Shah Nawaz had escaped to Afghanistan and subsequently married Afghan women.

Shortly after the one-year anniversary of Bhutto's death, Benazir and her mother were freed without explanation or ceremony. They returned to Karachi, and Benazir returned to politics. This time she was well aware that government officials watched her every move. To relieve the strain, Nusrat suggested that her daughter go to Larkana and see to the family lands. This was usually a man's job, but with her father dead and her brothers in hiding, Benazir had no choice. Actually, the diversion served her well, and the farmlands prospered under her management.

But the country was still under Zia's ever more strict control. After Chaudhry had completed his term in 1978 and would not accept another, Zia also took on the office of president. Thus he became the undisputed leader of Pakistan. He gave himself the power to dissolve the National Assembly at will. With no parliament, he set up a system called Majlis-e-Shoora. Its 284 members—said to be mostly intellectuals and journalists—were to serve as advisors to Zia.

Elections were set for 1980, but Nusrat and Benazir knew that it would take more strength than the PPP had to defeat Zia. They agreed to meet with the opposition party, the PNA. Out of the meeting came the Movement to Restore Democracy (MRD). Benazir was skeptical about joining with a former enemy, but there seemed no other way. The MRD set March 23 as a date for strikes and demonstrations throughout the country. But well before that date, thousands of MRD members, including Benazir, were arrested.

Once again, Benazir Bhutto was behind bars, this time in

a remote jail in the Thar Desert. It was a cagelike existence. She lost weight, and her ear infection continued to bother her. One day in April, she was abruptly transferred to a hospital, where she was told that she had uterine cancer. Terrified at the news, she underwent an operation. Later, still in jail, Benazir observed her twenty-eighth birthday.

With the election of President Ronald Reagan in 1980, the United States began sending aid to Pakistan once more. Millions of dollars suddenly began pouring into the country, and Zia became a hero. Newspapers now called him a statesman. Benazir heard the reports from her cell in disbelief.

In September 1981 Benazir was surprised to learn that she would be allowed to go to her sister's wedding in Karachi. For two days she was free, even though the authorities interrupted the wedding ceremonies on several occasions. She learned that her mother had been freed and was living in Europe. Then it was back to Benazir's small, dark cell. In late 1982, she was told she could go to Switzerland for treatment for her ear infection. Instead, she was placed under house arrest in Karachi once more.

What Benazir did not know during these months was that her friend Peter Galbraith was trying to get the United States to aid in her release. Finally, in June 1983, she was told that she could leave the country for ear surgery in Switzerland. She landed in Geneva in January 1984. An unbelieving Benazir Bhutto had been waiting for this moment for seven years.

CHAPTER FOUR

Prime Minister Once

THE DEATH OF BENAZIR'S FATHER, the most commanding presence in her life, gave her a new maturity and a new purpose. Her years under house arrest and in jail solidified her future. If politics had not been her main goal before, it was now. She vowed that her father's call for democracy in Pakistan would not die. She would be the nation's new leader.

PARTY HEAD IN EXILE

Although Benazir was allowed to leave Pakistan for Switzerland, she had to go to London for her ear surgery. It was performed successfully in late January 1984. Her mother joined her. She also met her friend Peter Galbraith once again. He suggested that she go to the United States and teach at Harvard. Benazir declined; she had to stay as close as possible to her country. She was determined to return one day. However, in March she did fly to Washington, D.C., where she spoke at the Carnegie Endowment for International Peace.

During her recuperation from ear surgery, Benazir traveled throughout England and to many parts of Europe. She spoke before the English parliament and to groups of Pakistanis in exile. Always, she protested the actions of Zia and exposed what she felt were human rights violations in her country.

Eventually, Zia did yield, not to Benazir's speeches but to pressure from the United States. The U.S. government strongly

Benazir waves to supporters as she campaigns against President Zia in late 1986.

suggested that Pakistan would benefit from national elections. Not willing to risk the loss of U.S. aid, Zia announced general elections for March 1985. At the same time, however, he made another announcement. Before the next elections, a referendum would be held in December. The people were supposedly asked to elect or reject Zia as president. Not surprisingly to most observers, the vote was reported as 95 percent for retaining him. Now he had the job officially for the next five years.

Zia won the general election in March 1985. Afterward, he said that the government would operate under civilian, not military, rule. But to Benazir's sadness, the same strict rules continued. Zia also passed the eighth amendment. It gave him so-called reserve powers to dissolve the National Assembly at will.

The results of the recent election were especially difficult for Benazir. Her chances of returning to her homeland seemed very far away. However, she continued to speak out against Zia. For example, she made a speech at Harvard to the Council on Foreign Relations.

When Benazir needed a break from politics, she looked to her family. She and her younger brother, Shah—now living with his Afghan wife in Cannes, France—were especially close. On one visit, he shocked Benazir by confiding that he was going to get a divorce. She scolded him and said that there had never been a divorce in the family. Later, she regretted her words. When Benazir, Nusrat, and Mir went to Cannes to see Shah in 1985, they found him dead on the living room floor. His wife, Rehana, said he had taken poison. The court ruled there was no evidence for the charge of murder. Their daughter Sassi was sent to the United States to live with relatives.

After Shah's death, Benazir decided she would take his body back to Pakistan for burial in the family grounds at Larkana. Her mother was nearly hysterical with fear that she would be killed. But Benazir

FOUL PLAY OR OVERDOSE?

Authorities already knew Shah Bhutto before his death in July 1985. Having left the country after their father's hanging, he and his older brother organized resistance to Zia's rule. Both brothers were convicted in absentia for involvement in a 1981 hijacking that resulted in the death of a Pakistani diplomat. Benazir and her mother insisted that Shah had been poisoned in Cannes, although French authorities disagreed. In June 1988 the French court said that Shah's wife, Rehana, must stand trial for not assisting someone in danger. But there was no charge of murder. Shortly afterward, Rehana left for the United States, where she joined her daughter.

was determined. She insisted that her brother be properly buried. Authorities did not release Shah's body until August. Crowds were heavy both at the airport in Karachi when they landed and at the burial grounds. The government neither interfered nor stopped the burial. But the next day, police came to arrest Benazir once again. This time even the U.S. government protested. Benazir was not released until November 3, when she returned to London.

HOMECOMING

Once again, Benazir traveled throughout Europe. She told her audiences that democracy had all but disappeared in her country. She spoke of Zia's ruthless measures. She said that freedom for women was limited. For example, women were disqualified from being witnesses in a murder trial. If a woman was murdered, her family would receive of half of the compensation they would have been awarded had the victim been male. Drugs were a major problem, as was the black market. The general unrest led to riots that broke out all over the country.

In January 1986, Benazir decided she had had enough. She told PPP members that she was going home. Although they acknowledged the danger, they agreed that the time seemed right. Zia claimed that civilian law now ruled Pakistan. If that was the case, how could he arrest her for peacefully returning to her country?

Benazir was not naïve about the dangers. There were many reports of threats to her life if she returned. But if these threats frightened her, she did not show it. She did, however, first make a trip to the United States, where she met with congressional leaders. She believed that their open support would help to protect her.

After eight years of exile, Benazir Bhutto returned to Pakistan in April 1986. As she recalled, "The eight-mile drive from the airport to the Minar-i-Pakistan in Iqbal Park usually takes fifteen minutes. On the unbelievable day of April 10, 1986, it took us ten hours." More than 2 million Pakistanis lined the streets to welcome her return on that day. The black, green, and red colors of the PPP waved everywhere. Benazir stopped to speak to the crowds in Lahore from the back of a truck. She spoke to them of democracy and a revolution that would oust Zia and his government.

Benazir continued to speak to crowds all over Pakistan during the next few months. Although there were constant threats against her life, she remained free. However, a number of PPP members were murdered, and others were shot at during public rallies. Benazir knew that the fight between the government and the PPP was really just beginning.

Pakistan celebrated independence day on August 14, 1986. As

Benazir prepared to speak publicly in Lahore, police appeared. Six people died in the riot, and many more were wounded. Benazir was arrested once again. This time she was put in solitary confinement at Landhi Borstal Jail outside Karachi. She remained there until September 10.

A SURPRISE ANNOUNCEMENT

Although the atmosphere was dangerous, Benazir Bhutto was again free to travel around her country, which she did. She no longer spoke of bringing down the government. She talked instead of building democracy and ending human rights violations. The PPP ran a membership drive, increasing its strength dramatically.

Then, in mid-1987, Benazir made a dramatic announcement. It had nothing to do with politics, and it surprised nearly everyone. She announced that she would marry a man she barely knew. Ironically, the daughter of a leader who prided himself on freedom for all had agreed to an arranged marriage. His name was Asif Ali Zardari.

Before his death, Bhutto had discussed a marriage between his daughter and Zardari, a man he had chosen. At the time, Benazir was shocked that her father would make such a suggestion. Two years younger than Benazir, Zardari was the son of a movie theater owner in Karachi. At the time, Zardari was a high school graduate with no interest in politics.

Why would a woman who had been brought up according to equal principles for both sexes agree to an arranged marriage in the old tradition? It might have been a political move. But, as Benazir later explained, it was the price she had to pay for a life in politics. She had no time to think of marriage while in exile. She had no chance to meet anyone or to marry during her years in jail or under arrest.

She had decided to devote her life to Pakistan and its people. What man would willingly take second place? In addition, she faced the fact that a single woman who enters politics in almost any country often unfairly faces disapproval. *The New York Times* had this report: "Ms. Bhutto's marriage to Mr. Zardari was arranged by her mother, a fact that Ms. Bhutto has often said was easily explained, even for a modern, highly educated Pakistani woman. To be acceptable to the Pakistani public as a politician she could not be a single woman, and what was the difference, she would ask, between such a marriage and computer dating?"

For all these reasons, Benazir agreed to marry a man she barely knew. Her mother assured her that love would come later. Seven days after the couple met, they became engaged. Benazir decided to go against the tradition of changing her last name to that of her husband. She said she had no intention of changing it after thirty-four years. She and Zardari were married in December 1987 during a ceremony for two hundred guests.

BHUTTO POWER RETURNS

General Zia was pleased with the announcement of Benazir's marriage. He thought it might signal the end of her involvement in politics. That did not happen, but Zia had a surprise announcement of his own. In May 1988, he suddenly dissolved the parliament and called for general elections in three months. PPP members cheered, but Benazir could only ask, *"Why?"*

Zia's actions are still unclear. The popularity of the PPP seemed to indicate that Benazir, as party leader, would become prime minister. Perhaps Zia thought that Benazir's marriage, along with the news that the couple was expecting their first child, would keep her out of

Benazir married Asif Ali Zardari in Karachi on December 18, 1987.

the political scene. He might have thought that the court would challenge Benazir's bid for office on the grounds that she was a woman.
But the constitution of 1973 declared either gender eligible for public
office—as did Zia's own constitution of 1985.

Zia instituted a voter registration clause. It said that all political
parties had to register with the government and provide lists of their
office holders and their accounts. That put the government in the
position of refusing participation to any party. This time Pakistan's
supreme court stood up and struck down the clause.

Then, suddenly, a fatal accident changed the future of Pakistan. On

THE GENERAL DICTATOR

Zia-ul-Haq (1924–1988) ruled Pakistan for eleven years. He was the third ruler in his nation's history to impose martial law. When he died in a plane crash in August 1988, several army generals died with him. So did the American ambassador to Pakistan and the head of the U.S. military aid mission to Pakistan. Although some believed the crash to be suspicious, the official report said it was an accident.

August 17, 1988, in the town of Bahawalpur in the Punjab, Zia-ul-Haq died in a plane crash. Benazir's main opposition disappeared.

MADAME PRIME MINISTER

Zia was gone, but the election was not over, and threats against Benazir's life continued. She stopped campaigning when her son, Bilawal, was born on September 21. Five days later she was back on the campaign trail. (The couple later had two daughters, Bakhtawar and Asifa.)

In the election of November 16, 1988, the PPP won the majority in the National Assembly of Pakistan. This was the country's first open election in more than a decade. According to Pakistani law, the person who headed the majority party was now the prime minister. Thus, under the bright lights of the Presidential Palace in Islamabad, Benazir Bhutto became the first woman—and the youngest person—ever to rule a Muslim nation. She was thirty-five years old. She later wrote about her feelings on that day:

This was not my moment, but the moment of all who had made sacrifices for democracy.

From the outset, Benazir said she wanted her time in office to signal both change and peace for Pakistan. She restored union rights and uncensored the media. For the first time, the press had access to political opponents of the government. She allowed groups committed to such causes as human rights to function freely. In an effort to improve relations with India, she invited its prime minister, Rajiv Gandhi, and his wife to Islamabad. Gandhi came from India's most prominent family. His mother, Indira, served fifteen years as prime minister and was assassinated in 1984. His grandfather, Jawaharlal Nehru, was independent India's first prime minister. Benazir decided that Pakistan would rejoin the British Commonwealth. She and Gandhi were scheduled for discussions on the topic, but Gandhi was assassinated in 1989. After that, relations between Pakistan and India turned sour again.

Benazir said that she wanted to introduce changes in Pakistan's government. But making any change after eleven years of largely military rule proved difficult. The military was watching her every move as they waited for a mistake and a chance for another coup. Benazir believed that right-wing groups might be anxious to defeat her solely because she was a woman. She also believed that some Muslim men wrongly interpreted the Qur'an as outlawing a woman in power.

In addition, there were severe problems outside the country. One was Pakistan's relationship with its neighbor, Afghanistan. The Soviets had invaded Afghanistan in 1979. At the time, Pakistani leadership would not recognize the Soviet-controlled government. When the Soviets left ten years later, the communist government was more firmly entrenched in Kabul. During the occupation period, however, Afghan rebels established their own government at Peshawar on the Pakistan border. Now Bhutto was forced to deal with both governments.

Early in her first term, Benazir encountered the work of terrorist Osama bin Laden. With $10 million, he funded a bill of no confidence in an unsuccessful attempt to overthrow her government. Bhutto later said she should have realized that bin Laden's intervention was "an early sign that his goal . . . was much broader than throwing the Soviet occupiers out of an Islamic country [Afghanistan]. It was actually a distorted vision of a caliphate [head of state] of Islamic states spanning Europe, Asia and Africa under the control of the religious extremists."

Another trouble spot for Benazir was the issue of women's rights in Pakistan. She campaigned loudly to improve women's health and civil rights. She vowed to raise the status of women by establishing women's development banks and by improving welfare and other programs. She promised that any laws that discriminated against women would be repealed under her administration. But none of these promises became realities. Nor was her government able to repeal the oppressive Hudood and Zina ordinances that Zia had set up. In both instances, her party explained that Benazir faced extreme opposition from the parties out of power and from right-wing religious groups.

BIN LADEN AND TERRORISM

Born in Saudi Arabia, Osama bin Laden is the acknowledged leader of the world's most infamous terrorist organization, al-Qaeda. (In Arabic, *Al-Qaeda* means "the base.") Outraged when the Saudi government allowed U.S. troops to be stationed in Saudi Arabia in 1991, he was expelled from the country due to his work against his government. He set up headquarters for al-Qaeda in the Sudan, and in 1996 he called for a declaration of war against the United States.

Immensely wealthy because of his family's construction business—and deeply radical—bin Laden was given a safe haven by Afghanistan's Taliban government. Today, with many lieutenants at his call, he rules a terrorist group that has surpassed such well-known organizations as the Irish Republican Army (IRA) and Hamas (the Islamic Resistance Organization). The U.S. State Department says that bin Laden is "one of the most significant sponsors of Islamic extremist activities in the world today." He is said to be partly (or wholly) responsible for at least four significant terrorist attacks: the U.S. World Trade Center bombing in New York City in 1993 and the collapse of its twin towers on September 11, 2001; the killing of nineteen U.S. soldiers in Saudi Arabia in 1996; and bombings in Kenya and Tanzania in 1998.

In 1990, Benazir dismayed India and other nearby countries when she signed an agreement that allowed China to build a nuclear power station in Pakistan. She affirmed that such power would never be used in war, but it made Pakistan's neighbors uneasy. A year earlier, Benazir had spoken to a joint session of the U.S. Congress and had promised that her country would not be turned into a nuclear power. In return, the United States awarded Pakistan increased economic and military aid.

CORRUPTION CHARGES

Opposition to Benazir's government was fierce from the beginning, but by late 1989 the criticism was out of control. During her time in office, she and her husband were accused of corruption, fraud, and money laundering (hiding the source of money). For instance, some people charged that Zardari made deals for Benazir's government and got 10 percent of each transaction for himself. Benazir repeatedly swore that the opposition had trumped up all these charges, and, indeed, she was never tried.

In November 1989, the National Assembly held a vote of no confidence. If the PPP had lost, Benazir would have been out of office. However, the party survived by just twelve votes. But the final blow came in 1990. For some time, a rift had been growing between Benazir Bhutto and Pakistan's military leaders. For instance, her government refused the army's call for increased powers to govern the Sindh region. Army commanders conveyed their displeasure over that and other contested points to President Ghulam Ishaq Khan. He used Zia's eighth amendment to dissolve parliament and call for an election. It was held in October. In her autobiography, Benazir said that the election was a fraud, and the military stacked the votes

ORDINANCES AGAINST WOMEN

The Hudood and Zina ordinances were instituted under Zia in 1979. These laws seemed designed to limit freedoms for women. Under the Hudood Ordinance, it was virtually impossible to prove an allegation of rape. To prove such a charge, a woman had to provide four adult males who witnessed the rape. That created a nearly impossible situation, since the four men would have had to testify that they just stood and watched the violent act and did nothing to stop it. Under the Zina Ordinance, sexual relations outside of marriage became a crime. In 2006, the National Assembly of Pakistan placed the charges of adultery and rape under the penal code.

against her. The military backed the Pakistan Muslim League (PML), which won 106 votes out of a possible 207. With the PPP no longer in power and her government dismissed, Benazir was no longer prime minister. She had been in office for two years.

Nawaz Sharif, a disciple of General Zia, was the leader of the PML. He now became head of the country. As leader of the opposition, Benazir Bhutto was on the outside once more.

CHAPTER FIVE

People Power in Pakistan

FROM Motahir Ahmed

(UNDER SUP
Muzaffar E
Malik

Prime Minister Twice

O N THE OUTSIDE LOOKING IN AGAIN—
all of Benazir's training from her father, all her
education, and all hers years in prison or exile had
netted her just two years in office. Was it time to throw up her
hands and settle for a quiet life away from politics? Never, said
the former prime minister. By now, she had earned a reputation
among party members for sheer determination. They called it
her chief attribute. However, Feisal Naqvi, a lawyer who knew
Benazir in Lahore, gave another reason for Benazir's never-
give-up attitude: "She believes she is the chosen one, that she
is the daughter of Bhutto and everything else is secondary."
Accordingly, the daughter of Bhutto merged into the background as the leader of the opposition party—and waited for a
second chance.

LEADER OF THE OPPOSITION

As leader of the opposition in the National Assembly, Benazir
fought against the changes instituted by the new government.
Censorship returned, as did a ban on the media and on student
unions. More religious parties now appeared in the new government. This meant that many more laws were challenged
as being anti-Islam. Sharif did introduce laws to alleviate poverty and social inequality. Opponents declared they were just
gimmicks, however. And Sharif ran into trouble with the so-
called Yellow Taxi Scheme. This plan was supposed to help

A political billboard featuring Benazir Bhutto
as Pakistan's first female prime minister

Pakistan's unemployed population by financing loans, but there was initial confusion over how much money would be available. Eventually it was straightened out, and about 40,000 households were financed with loans for taxis, buses, and trucks. Before long, however, the Sharif government was under attack for the way it managed the country's finances.

Sharif's policies encouraged Benazir to launch a series of verbal attacks condemning his money handling, among other things. In 1992 she was at the head of a march on Islamabad in an attempt to oust the prime minister. She even took sides with Khan, who had brought down her own government, in an effort to get rid of the current leadership. For that, Sharif's people called her a terrorist. But Benazir said it was merely a way of getting rid of an undesirable government—and, of course, restoring herself as leader. This win-by-any-method tactic is not unknown in countries around the world. It did not help Benazir win this time, but the resulting heated malice between the Sharif and Bhutto factions brought on riots and kidnappings around the country. The city of Karachi, in particular, was wracked with violence. When the unrest spread to the Punjab province, Sharif decided he had better postpone an intended trip to Japan.

During this period, Benazir herself survived an assassination attempt. As she was returning to her home in Larkana in 1992 someone fired a rocket at her car. Instead, it hit the police van that was protecting her, and six officers were killed.

Benazir also took her cause outside Pakistan. She made many speeches around the world, including the United States. Always, she stressed the need for a return of democracy to her country.

Even without Benazir's challenges, Sharif's government deteriorated. As prime minister. he seemed more interested in securing power for himself than in governing. His differences with President

Khan came to a boil over the choice of a new army chief of staff. The two men hurled charges at each other on television. Sharif even accused the president of trying to overthrow him. That was apparently the last straw. Khan did in fact dissolve Sharif's government with charges of poor administration and corruption. In July 1993 Moeen Qureshi became a caretaker prime minister. That led to the odd occurrence of having a head of state who was far more comfortable speaking English than the national language of Urdu.

In 1993 Pakistan held a general election. The PPP became the leading political party in the country. And once again, Benazir Bhutto became prime minister.

THE SECOND TIME AROUND

Benazir was in a good political position as she entered her second term of office. Her party was in strong control of the nation, including the important province of the Punjab. The new president was Farooq Leghari, with whom Benazir had a close political relationship. Indeed, Leghari promised that he would be a neutral president and let the prime minister do her job. From his words, it began to sound as though Bhutto might be the first prime minister in more than ten years to stay in office through a full term.

Even with those advantages, however, Benazir faced a more daunting challenge the second time around. The military was against her. Threats of terrorism were rampant. And Pakistan was nearly bankrupt. She did institute the Social Action Programme (SAP) to improve housing, education, and health services. Her government was also able to attract billions in foreign investment, most of it going to the generation of electric power in Pakistan.

Many observers cite the improvement in relations between

A smiling and confident Benazir casts her ballot in the 1993 election, which made her prime minister for the second time.

Pakistan and the United States as Benazir's main achievement in office. Relations between the two countries had deteriorated in 1994, when Nawaz Sharif had announced Pakistan's possession of nuclear weapons. In spring 1995 Benazir visited Washington, D.C. She presented a picture of an energized leader in control of a modern Islamic state. That September, as a result of her visit, the U.S. Senate passed the Brown amendment. It released millions of dollars worth of military equipment that Pakistan had already paid for and opened avenues for more economic aid.

An article in the *Independent* in Great Britain described the governing style of Benazir Bhutto in this way:

> In person she is charming, though her aides know her to be irascible and fiery at times. Sometimes she will interrupt herself to turn to her interrogator and ask, 'What do you think I should be doing?' And during her interviews she works hard to remain on message, carefully calibrating her language and themes. She will seamlessly manage to tell a right-wing British newspaper of her fondness for Mrs. Thatcher, the Indian media about her support for peace talks, and the American press of her loathing of fundamentalists. Like Mrs. Thatcher, she often resorts to the use of royal 'we,' though whether she is referring to herself, her party or the people of Pakistan is not always clear.

PAKISTAN AND NUCLEAR WEAPONS: A TIMELINE

1965   A nuclear reactor in Rawalpindi starts to function.

1979   The United States cuts off aid to Pakistan after learning it had secretly started to build a uranium-enrichment facility.

1984   President Zia says Pakistan has uranium capability only for peaceful purposes.

1985   The *Washington Post* claims Pakistan detonated a nuclear device in September.

1986   Zia says Pakistan has the right to obtain nuclear technology.

1987   Pakistan gets M-11 missiles and launchers from China.

1990   The United States claims Pakistan "cold-tested" a nuclear device; A. Q. Khan, father of Pakistan's nuclear bomb, gets the Man of the Nation award; the United States cuts off military and economic aid to Pakistan in October.

1996   In October, Bhutto calls for a conference in South Asia to deal with the nuclear arms issue.

1997   Nawaz Sharif says Pakistan has a right to nuclear weapons.

1998   Pakistan detonates six nuclear devices.

2008   Estimates of Pakistan's nuclear devices vary from forty to one hundred; Pakistan's president claims the devices are safe from Islamic militants.

While U.S.-Pakistan relations were improving under Benazir, relations between Pakistan and India were not. Each side accused the other of illegally fishing in the waters off Jammu and Kashmir, and there were many clashes between the two armies. For instance, in early 1996, nineteen Pakistanis were killed by Indian rockets, which also destroyed a mosque in a small village. Although there were meetings between the nations' prime ministers, relations did not improve, and the shelling continued on both sides.

CORRUPTION AND MISMANAGEMENT

In September 1996 police killed Mir Bhutto near his home in Karachi. This was especially heartbreaking news for Benazir since she and her brother recently had reconciled their political differences after many years apart. Benazir later claimed that Mir's murder was part of a plan to destabilize her government and to wipe out the Bhutto family. Her charges appeared to cast some blame for the murder on President Leghari, thus causing a rift between the two.

Both of Benazir's brothers were now dead. Her distress was complicated by the fact that her mother began showing the first indications of Alzheimer's, a disease that eventually takes away a person's memory and awareness. Uneasy about leaving her mother alone, Benazir took Nusrat along when she went to New York City in October to address the United Nations. In an impassioned speech, she appealed to the UN to help restore human rights and democracy both in Pakistan and in Jammu and Kashmir.

On November 4, 1996, in the United States, Bill Clinton was being reelected as the forty-second president. On the same day in Pakistan, President Farooq Leghari was using the powers of the eighth amendment. As a result, once again, Bhutto's government was

SWISS GOVERNMENT SAYS GUILTY

In 2003 the Swiss government found Benazir and Zardari guilty of money laundering. Zardari had earned the nickname of Mr. Ten Percent for his supposed kickbacks on government deals. It was claimed that a Swiss company paid them $10 million, which they deposited in Swiss accounts, in exchange for a contract in Pakistan. Benazir and her husband were ordered to pay $11 million to the government of Pakistan and were given six-month suspended jail terms. The trial took six months, and Benazir, insisting on her innocence, vowed to appeal.

Benazir always maintained that the corruption charges were politically motivated. Although many acknowledged her point, they also questioned just how Benazir and her husband acquired their wealth. Documents uncovered in Switzerland, Poland, France, and the United Kingdom posed awkward questions that the couple never fully answered.

dismissed. Some say that the dismissal came as a complete surprise to Benazir. Leghari charged Benazir with corruption and mismanagement. Shortly afterward, he had Benazir's husband, Zardari, arrested for Mir's murder. Although the murder charge was later dropped, Zardari was imprisoned for corruption and other offenses. He would not be set free until November 2004.

Benazir Bhutto was charged with a number of corruption cases, most of which were later cleared. She and her husband were also charged with money laundering; authorities claimed they stored state money in Swiss banks. Benazir, Zardari, and the PPP flatly denied all such charges.

Besides the charges of corruption, Benazir faced the claim of mismanagement. Many in Pakistan felt that she was lax in her handling of the religious situation in Karachi. A member of the Muhajirs, an ethnically mixed group of immigrants, charged that his people were victims of discrimination and ethnic cleansing. The violators, he said, were the elite Sindhis, which included the Bhutto family. He charged that the Sindhis comprised only about 2 percent of the population but controlled most of the nation. Many Pakistanis felt that Benazir's government did little or nothing to stop the campaign of violence against the Muhajirs.

Benazir's government was dissolved for the second time. Her husband was in jail. A once prosperous future looked bleak indeed. So, with her children and mother, Benazir packed some belongings and headed into exile again, this time in Dubai.

CHAPTER SIX

From Exile to Assassination

E VEN IN EXILE ON THE ARABIAN PENINSULA, Benazir did not give up thoughts of returning home and resuming leadership. She tried to keep in touch with PPP party members and often traveled to give lectures throughout Europe. She and her husband were reunited when he was released from prison in December 2004.

In early 2007 the United States invited Benazir to speak to President George W. Bush and Congress. Shortly afterward, she appeared on the BBC television program *Question Time* in Great Britain. At this point, she was openly speaking of her intention to return to Pakistan. That was a dangerous intention, however.

In 1999, three years after Benazir's government was dismissed, another coup d'état took place in Pakistan. This time former army chief of staff Pervez Musharraf took power. Once again, the military was in control.

When Musharraf was still president in 2002, he amended the constitution to ban prime ministers from serving more than two terms. That meant Benazir Bhutto could not run again. Even so, by mid-2007 the United States seemed to be pushing for an agreement between Musharraf and Benazir. Musharraf would remain president but step down as head of the military, and Bhutto, or someone she chose, would be named prime minister. Benazir seemed to agree. According to an Associated Press release in July 2007, she was going to return from exile and join Musharraf in a power-sharing

Benazir, her son Bilawal, and daughters — Bakhtawar (*left*) and Asifa — in exile in Dubai, December 2004

EXILE IN DUBAI

Dubai is the most populous of the seven loosely joined sheikhdoms that make up the United Arab Emirates (UAE). It is located on the southern coast of the Persian Gulf. The name of each sheikhdom and its main city—where the sheikh lives—are the same. The Al Maktoum dynasty has ruled Dubai since 1833. Its land is mostly desert, and until oil was discovered in 1958, the rest of the world knew little about Dubai. Many religious groups exist peacefully there, but the sheikhdom is mainly Muslim, most belonging to the Sunni branch.

arrangement. However, she ran into some criticism over the Red Mosque incident.

From July 3 to July 11 there was a battle between the Pakistani government and Islamic militants. It centered on the Lal Masjid (Red Mosque) in Islamabad. Fifty militants were captured, and 154 died. Afterward, there were reports that hundreds of young students were burned to death, and their remains were untraceable. In her remarks after the disaster, Benazir seemed to praise Musharraf for his handling of the incident. For that, many Pakistani leaders publicly criticized her.

In October 2007, Musharraf signed a national reconciliation ordinance that granted amnesty to most political leaders. This was the day before Musharraf faced a presidential poll in which he sought another five-year term. The ordinance opened the door for Benazir's return to Pakistan and politics.

HOMECOMING

After eight years in exile in Dubai and London, Benazir went home again. As she said in her autobiography:

> I . . . return to my homeland and once again lead the forces of democracy in electoral battle against the entrenched power of dictators, generals and extremists. This is my destiny. And as John F. Kennedy once said, 'I do not shrink from that responsibility, I welcome it.'

Benazir arrived in Karachi on October 18, 2007, to prepare for the national elections due in 2008. Near midnight on that date, the

Benazir's supporters await her return to Karachi in October 2007.

MUSHARRAF

Born in 1943, Pervez Musharraf, son of a diplomat, was raised in Pakistan and Turkey. He fought in the wars against India and was promoted to lieutenant general in 1995. Three years later he was promoted to general and became army chief of staff. The next year he was named chairman of the joint chiefs of staff committee.

Musharraf staged a bloodless coup in 1999 after Sharif tried to remove him. He promised to restore democracy in the country and assumed the title of president in 2001. Twice under his leadership, Pakistan's constitution was suspended. In 2002, a controversial referendum gave Musharraf five more years in power.

After the attack on the World Trade Center in New York City in 2001, the U.S. government sought Musharraf's support. Pakistan was one of the few countries in the world that acknowledged the existence of the Taliban, an Islamic guerrilla movement operating in Afghanistan. Musharraf had helped to get rid of the Taliban in Pakistan. Eventually, U.S. troops were sent into Afghanistan in hopes of finding terrorist leader Osama bin Laden among the Taliban forces. They were unsuccessful.

The target of much criticism in his country before and after Benazir's death, Musharraf announced his resignation in August 2008. His retirement set off wild celebrations in Pakistan.

streetlights went out, and the jammers used by her colleagues to secure broadcasting time suddenly stopped working. Benazir's security people called the police, but there was no response. Shortly after her car left Jinnah International Airport, two explosions took place in an apparent suicide bomb attack. After the first one, Benazir calmly told her people not to go outside, as she was certain another bomb would follow. In all, about 136 of Benazir's supporters died and at least 450 were wounded, including some 50 PPP security guards who had formed a human chain to protect her. Within minutes after the attack, police arrived to hose down the area.

Benazir did not openly blame Musharraf for the attack, even though he ordered no investigation of the incident, and even though she believed his allies had staged it. In a letter sent through diplomatic channels, she gave him the names of four people she thought were responsible. Musharraf never replied. When asked about her reaction to the near miss, Benazir commented,

" **I have no feeling. I go into a detachment, I start ticking off steps I have to do next.** "

The government said Benazir was responsible for the attack because she was campaigning in public. Musharraf claimed he had warned her to keep out of the public eye. His spokesman commented,

" **We don't want a dead Benazir on our hands. She'd be just another unlikely martyr that we don't need.** "

After the incident, Benazir went back to Dubai but returned in early November, this time to her home in Lahore. Cheering supporters greeted her. But just as she was about to speak at a political rally, she was placed under house arrest.

In a telephone interview with National Public Radio in the United States, Benazir declared that some four thousand policemen encircled her home, thus turning it into a prison. The following day, the government lifted the house arrest. Later that month, she filed papers for the upcoming January elections. At the same time, rival and former prime minister Nawaz Sharif returned from exile in Saudi Arabia with the intention of running again.

THE ASSASSINATION

Benazir Bhutto was aware of the dangers she faced, especially when speaking in public. However, she said she had a duty to face the people. After the October attack, the PPP asked Musharraf's government to provide security for Benazir. There was little response. Yet, as noted in an article for *Parade* magazine in 2007, "She just kept on without security, she didn't care about the personal danger. She was the bravest person I ever knew."

In the *Parade* article, Benazir was quoted as saying,

I am what the terrorists most fear. . . . We must be out on the streets, or the terrorists win.

At a campaign rally in Rawalpindi, Benazir waves to followers just moments before her assassination.

On December 27, 2007, Benazir, now fifty-four years old, spoke to party supporters at a spirited campaign rally. When she returned to her bulletproof car, she stood up to wave to the crowds through the sunroof. Shots rang out, and scattered explosives killed some twenty bystanders. A critically wounded Benazir was rushed to Rawalpindi General Hospital, less than 2 miles (3.25 km) away. She died on the operating table.

On the order of Benazir's husband, there was no autopsy. The hospital said she died from shrapnel wounds to the head, and aides confirmed the assessment. The doctors who treated her did not speak to the press. A spokesman from the Pakistan Ministry of Interior said she fractured her skull when she tried to duck back into the car after the blast. British detectives, whom the Pakistani government asked to investigate the killing, agreed.

Benazir's body was carried above a crowd of supporters from the hospital late that night. A Pakistan Air Force plane flew the body, as well as her husband and three children, to Sukkur. She was buried next to her father at the family mausoleum in Larkana District, Sindh. Thousands of supporters attended the ceremony. Like her father, Benazir Bhutto chose a life in politics, and died from the choice.

The true identity of Benazir's killers is still unknown, but there are many suspects. Some cite members of the al-Qaeda group, partly because these terrorists, led by Osama bin Laden, claimed responsibility some days after the assassination. Al-Qaeda's motive might have been that any instability in Pakistan would further the group's aims. According to Benazir some time before her death, she believed that an attack on her life would come from the Pakistani military officials who sided with Zia. Warlords on the Afghan border also have been singled out as possible instigators.

Immediately following the assassination, the nation endured much violence. Rioters took over. They burned cars and wrecked election offices. Said a retired Pakistani general, "Conditions in the country have reached a point where it is too dangerous for political parties to operate." Musharraf announced three days of mourning. At the same time, the Pakistani ambassador to the United States

Benazir's children and other family members mourn at her gravesite in the family mausoleum.

said publicly that Benazir had been provided with all the security she needed. Sharif called her death a tragedy for the country and said his Muslim League party would boycott the coming elections. The United Nations held an emergency meeting and loudly condemned the assassination. India's prime minister said he was deeply shocked. Great Britain's prime minister warned that terrorists—if indeed they had caused the tragedy—must not be allowed to take over Pakistan's

THE POLITICAL STATURE
OF ASIF ALI ZARDARI

Benazir Bhutto's husband, Asif Ali Zardari, was born in Kara-chi on July 26, 1955. He graduated from high school at the Ca-det College Petaro. His family is Shiite Muslim. Until his wife's death, many people regarded Zardari as a political liability for Benazir's party. He spent several years in jail in what some call trumped-up corruption charges.

In 1996, Zardari was charged with the murder of Benazir's older brother, but the charges were later dropped. After he was released from prison in 2004, Zardari kept a low profile. In the United States, he underwent medical treatment for diabetes and a spinal ailment. For all of their married life, Zardari kept in the background. He seemed to have no interest in politics.

politics. U.S. president George W. Bush called the act cowardly. On what would have been Benazir's next birthday, the Pakistani govern-ment pardoned all convicts on death row in her honor, and Islam-abad International Airport was renamed for her.

Three days after Benazir's death, her husband proclaimed him-self, along with his nineteen-year-old son, Bilawal, co-chairmen of the PPP. Benazir's political will, which she wrote after the October bombing, was made public two months after her death. In it, she asked that the party leadership be turned over to her husband because ". . . he is a man of courage and honor. . . . He has the political stature to keep our party united. "

In Zardari's new position, he joined forces with Sharif and other smaller political groups. The result was a big victory in the national elections in early 2008 and the unseating of Musharraf's Pakistan Muslim League party. In March and April, Zardari was cleared of all corruption charges.

After Musharraf resigned from the presidency, elections were held in September 2008. Asif Ali Zardari scored 281 votes out of a possible 426. In a remarkable passing on of power, Benazir's husband was now the president of Pakistan.

CHAPTER SEVEN

Destiny's Family

I N 1988 BENAZIR BHUTTO PUBLISHED HER autobiography, *Daughter of Destiny*. In it, she said that she did not choose her life; it chose her. Whichever way, that choice was politics. And politics has not proven to be healthy for the Bhutto family. Benazir's father, Zulfikar Ali Bhutto, was hanged in 1979. Of the four children born to him and his wife Nusrat, only the second daughter—Sanam, called Sunny—is alive today. She lives in London with her two children.

Benazir, who was assassinated in 2007, outlived both her brothers. Her younger brother, Shah Nawaz, was found dead under mysterious circumstances in France in 1985 at age twenty-seven. Benazir believed he had been poisoned. His wife now lives in the United States.

Her older brother, Mir Murtaza, was shot to death in Karachi in September 1996 at age forty-two. After his father was hanged, he left for Afghanistan and began a militant branch of the PPP, which his father had founded. He was elected to the Sindh government in 1993, and he accused his sister of corruption. In what was said to be a police ambush, he and six supporters were shot. Benazir's government arrested all the survivors and witnesses. However, Mir's daughter, Fatima, criticized what she called her aunt's role in the death of her father.

Bilawal, one of Benazir's three children, is a bookish Oxford student who has spent about half his life in England and Dubai. According to Zardari, he is destined to lead the

Ali Zardari, who became Pakistan's president in September 2008, is shown next to a picture of his assassinated wife.

Pakistan government. According to an article in *Time* magazine, Bilawal enjoys sports, including squash, target-shooting, swimming, and horseback-riding.

Both of Benazir's daughters, Bakhtawar and Asifa, also study abroad. In 2009 Bakhtawar, a student at the University of Edinburgh in Scotland, wrote a rap song to honor her mother. It is titled "I Would Take the Pain Away."

THE BHUTTO LEGACY

A January 2008 article in *Time* magazine describes Benazir and her government in this way:

> Benazir Bhutto was a brave, gutsy, secular and liberal woman. But she was a central part of Pakistan's problems, not a solution to them.

Acknowledging that Benazir was a liberal and pro-Western leader, the article declares her actions to be often far from democratic. She kept silent when President Musharraf tried to hamstring the Pakistan supreme court. She was silent when he exiled Sharif to Saudi Arabia, thereby removing her chief rival. And, in perhaps her most undemocratic action, she handed over the head political position of the PPP to her husband without consulting party members.

Some of her critics call Benazir Bhutto an inept administrator. Although she spoke earnestly about liberal causes such as the improvement of women's rights, for all her rhetoric, her government passed no legislation toward that end during either of her premierships. When she left office, there was no fundamental change in the status of women in Pakistan or any progress in addressing women's issues.

Yet most would agree that Benazir Bhutto was, as the *Time* article states, a brave and gutsy woman. She had to know that she was in danger at all times, if only because she was charting a new course as an Islamic woman trying to lead an Islamic nation. Benazir had the talent for attracting huge crowds. She said she would bring a new beginning for her country. She promised a better tomorrow, a chance for Pakistan to become a truly modern, progressive state.

Benazir Bhutto did not deliver on those promises. Perhaps no one in her position could have. She may have been born into a social class that made her feel more competent than most others. But that competence stood against great odds. Benazir gave her country hope but not results. Therefore, some Pakistanis regard her years in office as a failure. Others may remember her fierce independence, especially in the last year of her life. Whether she was fighting because of a true belief in justice or whether she was fighting to uphold her family name, she did risk death many times. For that alone, many regard Benazir Bhutto as a martyr for democracy.

TIMELINE

1947	Pakistan gains independence
1953	Benazir Bhutto born into wealthy family in Karachi, June 21
1963	Benazir attends boarding school in Murree
1967	Ali Bhutto founds Pakistan Peoples Party (PPP)
1969	Benazir enters Radcliffe College, Harvard University
1971	Ali Bhutto named president of Pakistan
1973	Benazir graduates from Radcliffe, enters Oxford University
1976	Benazir graduates from Oxford
1977	Ali Bhutto overthrown
1979	Ali Bhutto hanged, April 3; Benazir under house arrest
1984	Benazir has ear surgery in London
1985	Brother Shah poisoned

1986	Benazir returns to Pakistan from exile to head PPP, April
1987	Benazir marries Asif Ali Zardari, December 18
1988	Benazir becomes first female and youngest prime minister of a Muslim state, December 2
1989	Her government dismissed for corruption, August 6
1993	Benazir becomes prime minister again, October 19
1996	Brother Mir Murtaza dies in battle with police; Benazir's government dismissed, November 2; she goes into exile in Dubai
1998	Pakistan conducts nuclear tests
1999	Benazir found guilty of corruption while in exile, April 14
2007	Benazir returns to Pakistan to campaign; escapes suicide bombing, October 18; Assassinated in Rawalpindi, December 27
2008	Benazir's husband becomes president of Pakistan, September 20

SOURCE NOTES

Boxed quotes unless otherwise noted

CHAPTER 1

p. 10, par. 3, Benazir Bhutto, *Daughter of Destiny: An Autobiography* (New York: Harper, 2008), p. 29.

p. 12, par. 2, *Daughter of Destiny*, p. 37.

p. 13, par. 1, *Daughter of Destiny*, p. 36.

CHAPTER 2

p. 24, par. 1, www.elections.com.pk/candiatedetails.php?id=6884, p.3.

p. 27, par. 1, *Daughter of Destiny*, p. 49.

p. 30, par. 1, Owen Bennett Jones, *Pakistan: Eye of the Storm* (New Haven, CT: Yale University Press, 2002), p. 147.

CHAPTER 3

p. 33, par. 2, www.elections.com.pk/candiatedetails.php?id=6884, p. 4.

p. 34, par. 2, *Daughter of Destiny*, p. 71.

p. 36, par. 1, *Daughter of Destiny*, p. 73.

CHAPTER 4

p. 52, par. 3, "Three million received Bhutto on return in 1986," www.rediff.com/news/2007.Oct/18bhutto.htm

p. 54, par. 1, Jane Perlez, "Benazir Bhutto, 54, Lived in Eye of Pakistan Storm," *New York Times*, December 28, 2007, p. A12.

p. 57, par. 1, *Daughter of Destiny*, p. 392.

p. 58, par. 2, *Daughter of Destiny*, p. 405.

p. 59, par. 2, http://news.bbc.co.uk/l/hi/world/south_asia/155236.stm

CHAPTER 5

p. 63, par. 1, Perlez, "Benazir Bhutto," p. A12.

p. 67, par. 1, Andrew Buncombe, "Benazir Bhutto: Pakistan's former prime minister has risen again," www.independent.co.uk/news/people/profiles/benezir-bhutto-pakistans-former-prime-minister-has-risen-again-401070.html (article printed September 1, 2007).

CHAPTER 6

p. 75, par. 1, *Daughter of Destiny*, p. xx.

p. 77, par. 1, "Behind the Assassination of Benazir Bhutto," www.parade.com/benazir-bhutto/assassination.html, January 21, 2009, p. 1.

p. 77, par. 2, "Behind the Assassination," www.parade.com, p. 1.

p. 78, par. 2, "Behind the Assassination," www.parade.com, p.1.

p. 78, par. 4, "Behind the Assassination, www.parade.com, p. 1.

p. 80, par. 4, "Behind the Assassination, www.parade.com, p. 1.

p. 82, par. 1, *Daughter of Destiny*, p. 433.

CHAPTER 7

p. 86, par. 1, "The Cursed Dynasty," *Time*, January 14, 2008, p. 48.

p. 86, William Dalrymple, "Martyr without a Cause," *Time*, January 14, 2008, p. 47.

FURTHER INFORMATION

BOOKS

Bhutto, Benazir. *Daughter of Destiny: An Autobiography.* New York: Harper, 2008.

L'Homme, Erik. *Tales of a Lost Kindgom—A Journey into Northwest Pakistan.* New York: Enchanted Lion Books, 2007.

Porterfield, Jason. *Islamic Customs and Culture.* New York: Rosen, 2009.

Siddiqui, Haroon. *Being Muslim.* Anansi, CA: Groundwood, 2006.

WEBSITES

Islam
Introduction to and history of the Islamic religion.
www.religioustolerance.org/islam.htm

K 2
History and facts about the world's second-tallest mountain, located in Pakistan.
www.k2news.com/k2history.htm

Pakistan
Travel information for touring this beautiful South Asian land.
www.lonelyplanet.com/pakistan

BIBLIOGRAPHY

BOOKS

Bhutto, Benazir. *Daughter of Destiny: An Autobiography*. New York: Harper, 2008.

_____. *Reconciliation: Islam, Democracy, and the West*. New York: Harper/Collins, 2008.

Choudhury, Golam W. *Pakistan: Transition from Military to Civilian Rule*. Essex, UK: Scorpion, 1988.

Jones, Owen Bennett. *Pakistan: Eye of the Storm*. New Haven, CT: Yale University Press, 2002.

Musharraf, Pervez. *In the Line of Fire: A Memoir*. New York: Free Press, 2006.

Talbot, Ian. *Pakistan: A Modern History*. New York: St. Martin's, 1998.

ARTICLES

"Obituary: Benazir Bhutto," BBC News, http://news.bbc.co.uk/2/hi/south_asia/2228796.stm

Perlez, Jane, and Victory Burnett. "Benazir Bhutto, 54, Lived in Eye of Pakistan Storm," www.nytimes.com/2007/12/28/world/asia/28bhuttocnd.html.

Robins, Simon, "Why Pakistan Matters," *Time*, January 14, 2008, pp. 42-48.

"Timeline: The Turbulent Life of Benazir Bhutto," www.npr.org/templates/story/story.php?storyId=17650276

Waraich, Omar. "The Moment: 9/20/08 Islamabad," *Time*, October 6, 2008.

INDEX

ABOUT THE AUTHOR

CORINNE J. NADEN is a former children's book editor and U.S. Navy journalist, who has written more than ninety books for children and young adults. She lives in Tarrytown, New York.